WHITE GIRL PROBLEMS?
NAH, IT'S EVERYONE

- By Tre Chado

DEDICATION

For my Daughters' who knows their purpose is not on layaway.
For the ones who were told to be quiet, sit still, and survive.
This one's for you. The Black Sheeps Of Society.
You were never the problem. We all have issues.
Keep Moving Forward, Find Your Purpose.

COPYRIGHT

CHAPTER LIST:

1. The Girl Who Thought Purpose Was for Skylar

2. Broke People Don't Take Sabbaticals, They Take Naps

3. Therapy? Girl, I Got Cousins and Gospel Music

4. Not Me Journaling and Crying in the Break Room

5. Finding Myself in the Hood, at the Bus Stop

6. When You Don't Even Know You're Lost

7. Sometimes Purpose Look Like a Messy Bun and an Attitude

8. I Thought My Purpose Was Just to Be a Bad Example

9. White Girl Problems? Nah, It's Everyone

CHAPTER 1: THE GIRL WHO THOUGHT PURPOSE WAS FOR SKYLAR

There once was a girl who thought purpose was a personality trait white girls inherited with their oat milk and an unbalanced check book.

She didn't say it out loud, but deep in the corner of her chest, tucked behind all the to-do lists and fake smiles, that thought sat cross-legged like it paid rent. Because every time she saw somebody *finding themselves,* it looked like a white girl with limited funds, free time, and a flight to somewhere with turquoise water.

Skylar would get dumped by her accountant boyfriend, and suddenly she's *healing loudly in Costa Rica.* Madison gets passed up for a promotion and poof—she's on a mountain with a burning bundle of sage and a nose ring she didn't have last week. Lindsay leaves her man, and next thing you know, she's barefoot in a garden whispering to cucumbers.

They all had names like breezes and brunch menus, and they were all *walking in purpose.*

Meanwhile, this girl? She's walking to the bus stop, wondering if she left the curling iron on and how she's going to stretch one pack of chicken over three days.

Ain't nobody ever told her she could find herself. Where she came from, her people didn't do *finding.* They did surviving. They knew how to stretch meals, stretch money, and stretch their backs carrying everybody else's burdens. But they didn't stretch out in the grass, staring at the sky, asking, *"After yoga, should I go to Pilates today?"*

And If you ever thought about slowing down to think, somebody hit you with the, *"Must be nice."* Or worse, *"You got time to sit there, you must not want it bad enough."*

So she assumed finding purpose wasn't for her. That it was something you could only afford after your problems got small and your bills got paid. Something soft girls with emotional support dogs and backup savings accounts did between hot yoga and therapy sessions.

She figured she missed the train. Probably never had a ticket to begin with.

But late one night, while the house was still and the microwave hummed its third reheat of the day, she felt something. Not dramatic. Not spooky. Just a tug. A tiny knock on the inside.

She paused, spoon half-full to her mouth, and listened to nothing in particular. It was just… quiet. Too quiet. That's when it came. A whisper without sound. A question without words.

What if?

That's all it said. Just, what if? What if you weren't just born to pay bills, make dinner, and fake a laugh? What if the ache in your chest was a map, not a malfunction?

She blinked. Shook it off. Told herself she was just tired. But the knock didn't stop. It showed up the next day while she was folding laundry. It crept in while she was watching reruns. It curled up at her feet while she scrolled through Skylar's post about *"rediscovering wholeness in Portugal."*

She started side-eyeing everything. Why am I still here? Why do I keep choosing people who don't choose me? Why do I laugh when I want to scream?

She didn't tell anyone. How do you explain that something invisible is tapping on your spirit? That maybe, just maybe, you're being called by something bigger, older, holier than your excuses?

But she wasn't ready to believe that yet. Not fully. She still had dishes in the sink and doubts in her head. She still thought Skylar had the secret. She still wasn't sure this... thing... this purpose thing... could be hers.

So she carried the question like a pebble in her shoe—irritating and relentless. Impossible to ignore and oddly comforting. Because even if she didn't have the answer, at least now she knew there was a question. She didn't know where it would lead. Didn't know how long it would take. All she knew was this:

Something had started. Something had shifted—and she couldn't shift back.

And from that day on, no matter how loud the world got, she couldn't ignore that silent knock.

CHAPTER 2: BROKE PEOPLE DON'T TAKE SABBATICALS: THEY TAKE NAPS

She didn't pack a suitcase. Didn't buy crystals. Didn't even Google *"how to find your purpose"* because her Wi-Fi was spotty and she had already used her hotspot helping her cousin stream reruns of *Living Single*.

But still, she was on a journey.

Not one with a map or cute matching loungewear. More like the kind where you leave your house to get dish soap and somehow end up outside talking to a stranger in your neighborhood about their cat's anxiety disorder while holding a half-melted popsicle.

She started small. Watching certain individuals.

Not in a creepy way, but she was curious. What made some folks glow like they knew where they were going, while others moved like their batteries were low?

First stop: Ms. Darlene from the corner store. Sixty-seven years old. Hair dyed redder than a fire truck in July. Her purpose? Selling pickles and reminding folks they're blessed, even if they forget.

"Baby, your purpose don't have to be fancy. It just gotta fit," she said, bagging a loaf of bread and a Slim Jim. *"Mine was to keep this corner lit and remind you to mind yo business."*

Next: her old high school art teacher. Ran into him at the dollar store buying glitter. *"I make collages now,"* he said, dead serious. *"People send me their heartbreak stories, and I glue them into something pretty."*

She asked, *"You think that's purpose?"*

He smiled. *"I think anything that makes pain useful is purpose."*

That one stuck.
Then came the barber. A mama at the bus stop. A girl outside the bodega selling snake oils. A dude in an apron who blessed every sandwich he wrapped.

Purpose was showing up in places she never expected. Not loud. Not always poetic. But it was there in folks doing what they were made for—even if they didn't get a plaque or followers for it.

She started writing it down. Like it mattered. Notes on napkins. Thoughts in the margins of overdue bills.

Purpose can be in the way you fry fish.
Purpose might be how you say hello.
Purpose ain't a destination; it's a decision.

She even started people-watching on purpose. Not to judge. To learn. She'd sit on the bench outside the laundromat with a bag of hot chips and observe the world like it was trying to tell her something.

She watched a teenage boy help an elderly woman carry laundry and not ask for a dime. A woman in scrubs laughed so hard she dropped her drink, then picked it up and kept laughing.
She started noticing the sacred in the small.

The woman humming while sweeping hair in the salon. The man talking to his plants on the balcony. The elder who wore her Sunday hat on a Tuesday just because it made her feel like royalty.

That's when it hit her: maybe purpose didn't knock. Maybe it whispered. Maybe it was hiding in plain sight, waiting for her to slow down and see it.

She tried things too. Real small, secret stuff.

One morning, she made oatmeal and arranged banana slices in a smiley face. Just because. She complimented the grumpy lady at the DMV. She let her niece braid a chunk of her hair and said, *"Wow, I feel like a Queen."*

Each time she did something with full presence, it felt like a piece of herself clapped in approval.

It wasn't dramatic.
It didn't pay bills.

It didn't solve world hunger.
But it *felt* right.

And she began to believe that maybe purpose could live in moments too quiet for applause.

CHAPTER 3: THERAPY?
GIRL, I GOT COUSINS
AND GOSPEL MUSIC

She started walking slower. Not because she was tired, but because she wanted to *see.* And people, when you really look at them, become stories. Whole novels walking around in beat-up shoes and corner store hoodies. She saw a man dance while sweeping his porch. Just a little shimmy. Nobody watching. He had headphones in, and his broom was his mic stand.

She saw a mother whisper affirmations to her daughter while parting her hair. *"You are beautiful. You are worthy. You are the sun, baby girl."* She passed a boy drawing stars with chalk on the sidewalk and asked him what he was doing. *"Making a galaxy where everyone is satisfied,"* he replied.

That night, she couldn't sleep. Her bed felt like too much silence and not enough story.
She sat up, grabbed a crumpled grocery receipt, and scribbled:

Maybe purpose is just letting the world know you see it and letting it see you back.

She had nothing against therapy. She just ain't have the time. Or the money. Or the insurance. And even if she did, where was she supposed to find a therapist who understood why her family kept plastic on the furniture and trauma in the basement?

Nah. Her therapy came in other forms.

It came in her cousin Gloria's kitchen at 7:00 p.m. Friday at some odd degrees in the nineties, two wine coolers in, both of them wearing bonnets and eating porridge out of mixing bowls.

"Girl, that man ain't even cute in the daylight," Gloria said, snatching the remote like it was part of her healing process.

That's when she knew she was being seen.

Not analyzed. Not broken down into attachment styles and inner-child diagrams.

Just seen.

Because Gloria, with her chipped acrylics and prophetic one-liners, had a master's degree in *Don't Let That Man Steal Your Glow*.

And gospel? Whew. That wasn't background music. That was CPR.

Sometimes she'd put on Mary Mary and cry for reasons she couldn't name. Sometimes she shouted with Kirk Franklin like she was trying to evict a demon through her vocal cords. And sometimes she just lay on the floor, hands across her chest, while the organ did the talking. There was healing in the harmony. There was therapy in the tambourine. There was a breakthrough in that one Clark Sisters riff that felt like a scream wrapped in a hymn.

She didn't call it therapy. She called it surviving with a soundtrack. And yet, deep down, she sometimes wondered if real therapy could've helped.

But every time she'd get close to scheduling something, life would tap her on the shoulder and yell, "*Message*." Somebody would need something. A bill would surprise her. Her own body would betray her with a stress cold or a headache that felt like unpaid rent.

So she went back to her usual methods: Cousins. Gospel. Crying in the bathtub with a mango-scented candles lit like it was a holy vigil. Using Alchemist Tinq's soaps.

She had a system.

Mondays were "*Mind Your Business and Drink Water*" days.
Wednesdays were "*Tell Gloria Everything That's Bothering You Without Naming Names*" nights.
Fridays? "*Gospel, Grease, and Gratitude*" sessions.

She'd deep-condition her hair, blare some Kirk Franklin, and say out loud everything she made it through that week—it didn't matter where Friday found her. Her goal was peace—and Yahweh always met her there.

"*Didn't cuss out that coworker? Look at Yahweh.*"
"*Made dinner outta canned beans and leftover rice? Multiply, Elohim!*"
"*Didn't text that man back? That's growth, not ghosting. Discern-*

ment"

One day she ran into an old friend from school, the kind who posts filtered peace quotes and says things like *"holding space"* unironically. *"You know, you should try somatic healing,"* the girl said, sipping an $8 tea. *"I've been doing trauma release through breathwork."*

Sis blinked.

"I've been doing trauma release through keeping my house quiet and not dating men who bring chaos."

The girl didn't laugh. But she did nod like she understood, which, weirdly, helped.

Maybe they weren't so different. One paid for breathwork; the other screamed into pillows and did dishes while humming "*Take Me to the King.*"

Healing was healing.

She began to realize something: *she had always been doing the work.* She just hadn't named it therapy because nobody gave her language for it. Nobody said, when you sit on your porch and let your toes touch the grass, that's grounding. Nobody told her that talking to your auntie for two hours about everything and nothing is called community-based emotional regulation.

They called it *"girl talk."*
They called it *"venting."*

They called it *"laughing to keep from crying."*

But it was therapy. Unpaid, unlicensed, and soaked in hot grease and hair oil—but therapy nonetheless, with zero confidentiality.

And once she accepted that, she started treating it like what it was. She showed up to her own healing like it was an appointment. She made space to feel things. To talk to herself out loud without shame. To let the gospel *be* gospel—not background music, but a balm.

She started journaling again. Nothing fancy. Just scribbles on the back of bills. A sticky note on the fridge that read:

"Today I didn't fall apart. That's enough."

She made playlists for her moods:

Songs to Cry in the Shower 2
Praise Breaks for Petty Days
Don't Text Him Anthems, Volume 3

And she started realizing… maybe she didn't need to *"find"* herself like she was lost. Maybe she had just been muffled. Drowned out. Told that real healing came with a co-pay and a softly lit office.

But her healing had always lived in her. In her voice. Her cousins. Her gospel. Her resilience.

In the way she knew when to crack a joke to keep her sister from crying.

In the way she handed someone a plate without asking if they were hungry.

In the way she danced in the mirror on days she didn't feel cute while taking a selfie just to post it on MySpace with a caption that read, *"Feeling cute, might delete later."* All to remind herself what divine looked like in motion —and that she was made in Yahweh's image.

CHAPTER 4: NOT ME JOURNALING AND CRYING IN THE BREAK ROOM

She told herself it was allergies. Because what else do you say when you're hunched over behind the vending machine in a break room that smells like microwave fish, in full view, trying to hold it in by scribbling into a $3.50 notebook with tears you didn't plan for?

It started with the pen.

One of those cheap, smooth-writing, glide-across-the-page pens. She bought it days ago on impulse at the dollar store, along with a notebook —pink cover, gold letters that read:

You Got This, Queen.

She didn't feel like a queen. She felt like a folding chair at a cook-out, overused and about to snap.
But that morning, something made her throw the notebook in her tote bag next to her keys, lotion, and the same granola bar she kept forgetting to eat.

And now, here she was. She had finally made it to the bathroom

Fourth stall on the left, sitting on an overturned mop bucket, writing like her sanity depended on it. *"I don't know what I'm doing. I'm tired. Not sleepy tired, bone tired. The kind of tired where even your dreams feel like errands."*

She stared at the words.

They looked like somebody else wrote them. Somebody braver. Somebody who wasn't always trying to make it sound prettier.

She flipped back and titled the page:

This Ain't a Breakdown, It's a Breakthrough.

Because if she called it what it really was, she'd scare herself.

Her coworkers thought she was the strong one. The *"hold it down"* girl. The funny one who made TikToks in the bathroom mirror and kept the team chat alive with memes.

Nobody knew she kept a sticky note inside her locker that said, *Just get through lunch.* That was her version of affirmations. Not *I am worthy.* Not *I radiate divine energy.* Just:

Make it to 12:30 and try not to cuss nobody out.

Sometimes she didn't even eat during lunch. Just sat in her car with the seat back, talking to Yahweh like He was her homeboy on the line.

"Hey, I know You busy parting seas, building universes, and whatnot, but I need You to part this mood and decimate these obstacles I'm in."

Later that day, back in the break room, it was the journal that caught her. Not the vending machine. Not the ache behind her eyes. Then it hit her—she'd been holding back her words her whole life.

She wrote about the coworker who always touched her hair without asking. She wrote about pretending to laugh at jokes she didn't find funny. She wrote about how nobody ever asked her what she wanted to be growing up, only what job she could get that came with benefits.

And she wrote, for the first time, about the weight. Not her physical weight. The weight of being *"the one."* The reliable one. The forgiving one. The one who smiles when she's bleeding internally.

She wrote until her hand cramped. Until her heart loosened its fist. Until something inside her sighed like it had been waiting.

Then the door creaked. Somebody walked in. She wiped her face and shoved the notebook into her bag like a teen caught texting during church.

"You good?" they asked.
She smiled. The one with all teeth and no truth.
"Yeah, girl, just whew, this job!"
They laughed.

And just like that, she put the mask back on. But under it, something had shifted.

Later that week, she started bringing the notebook everywhere. Called it her *"paper therapist."* Every break, she'd sneak in a few lines:

"I said 'I'm fine' seven times today and meant it zero."
"Why do I say yes so much? Who taught me that love is earned through exhaustion?"
"Is it normal to cry at a commercial for allergy meds?"

She wasn't trying to be poetic. She just needed to see herself somewhere. Needed to create a space that didn't require her to perform.

And little by little, her journal became that space.
She started leaving notes for herself. Sticky notes in her purse:

"Girl, you've survived worse."

Reminders on her bathroom mirror:

"You are not too much. They just ain't enough."
She even started a *"praise jar"* at home—little folded slips with anything worth celebrating:

Didn't cuss out the rude lady at the bank.
Took a walk instead of doom-scrolling.
Actually drank water today—look at Yahshua's influence!

One day, while journaling in the break room, she wrote,

"I'm not broken. I'm bruised, I'm tired, and I need a nap, but I'm not broken."

She stared at that sentence. Underlined it. Then wrote it again.

<u>*"I'm not broken. I'm bruised, I'm tired, and I need a nap, but I'm not broken."*</u>

That day, she didn't cry. She just exhaled. A real one. The kind of exhale that sounds like a release and a prayer had a baby.

The thing she was searching for still wasn't "found." She didn't wake up glowing or start making smoothies and buying herbs. She still had bad days. Still yelled at her phone when it froze. Still ran out of clean socks more than a grown woman should.

But she had a journal. And in it, she had proof. Proof that she felt things deeply. Proof that she was trying. Proof that even when she thought she was spiraling, she was actually peeling back the layers to find her core.

And that core? Wasn't soft like Skylar's beach retreats. Wasn't clean like Pinterest boards. It was raw. Holy. Human.

Her purpose wasn't in a breakthrough session or a seven-step plan. It was in her honesty. Her humor. Her pages of proof.

By the end of the month, she had filled three notebooks. She gave them names like they were best friends:

Volume 1: "I'm Not Crying, You're Crying"
Volume 2: "This Job Can't Kill Me if I Quit First"
Volume 3: "I'm Still Here... And Kinda Funny With It"

She thought about throwing them away once. But she was scared someone would find them, read them, and see through all the armor.

Then she realized if anybody found them, they wouldn't find weakness.

They'd find survival. With margin notes. And a few tear stains.

CHAPTER 5: FINDING MYSELF IN THE HOOD, AT THE BUS STOP

She didn't need a retreat in Sedona. She had the route #80 bus stop on East and 11th. Right in front of the auto parts store with the cracked window that had a sign saying, *"getting fixed next week"* since Obama's first term.

That corner? Her sanctuary. Her watchtower. Her seat at the bus stop, staring into the theater of humanity.

She didn't even realize it at first.

She just stood there most mornings, waiting for the bus with her headphones in, pretending to listen to music when really she was listening to the neighborhood talk to her.

People told on themselves in the way they waited. Some paced. Some slumped. Some sighed like they'd been holding it in for years. But all of them were trying. Just trying.

And she was one of them.

There was Miss Wanda, the unofficial mayor of the block. Her pushcart was full of plastic bags. She knew everybody's name and their business, whether they told her or not.

"You look tired, baby," Miss Wanda said one day, popping sunflower seeds and sipping a blue Slushy at 7:33 in the morning. *"You carrying something that ain't yours."*

It wasn't a question. It was a spiritual read.

She didn't answer. Just blinked back the tears and nodded like she was agreeing with the weather. Because truthfully, she *was* carrying things. Old shame. Other people's expectations. A version of herself she didn't even believe in anymore.

Then there was Melvin—young dude with locs and a gold tooth that caught the sunlight when he smiled. Sold mixtapes and loose cigarettes, but also gave the best relationship advice on the block. *"You gotta stop thinking your loyalty gon' teach him how to love you right,"* he told her one morning, no introduction. While lighting a cigarette like he wasn't even talking to her.

She thought, *"I wasn't even thinking about my ex. I was just tying my shoes."*

A few feet away there was the older woman with the walker who blessed every bus driver. It didn't matter if they were late, rude, or smelled like boiled ham. She'd grab their hand and whisper, *"You're doing better than you think."*

That woman changed her.

If somebody on a fixed income, walking with a prosthetic, could still pass out blessings like peppermints, what was her excuse?

She started showing up to the bus stop early. On purpose. Not to catch the bus, but to catch life.

To watch the dance of the day begin. To see how the neighborhood breathed.

Kids with uneven braids and sticky fingers racing each other. Men arguing about who the best rapper alive is again and again. Women swapping Tupperware and wisdom. A pigeon with a limp that refused to be left out.

Every part of it pulsed with truth. With survival. With a kind of purpose she hadn't seen in church sermons or YouTube clips—but one that felt familiar in her bones.

One day, she brought a notebook. Started writing again. This time, she didn't write about what she lacked. She wrote what she saw:

"The old man said his back hurt, but smiled anyway."
"A girl in a red hoodie just sang a whole love song to herself."
"Two strangers laughed like cousins today. Are they related? I don't know."

She started calling it *"Hoodalations,"* a blend of "hood" and "revelations."

Not because they were profound to anyone else, but because they were *real.*

Unfiltered. Sacred. Free.

Then came the morning she saw her reflection in the auto parts store window. Not just her face, but her fullness.

The curve of her hip, the set of her jaw, the way she stood like she *meant* to be there.

And she thought, *"Oh. There I am."*

No filter. No edit. No comparison to Skylar and her oat milk spiritual awakenings.

Just her.

Messy bun. Ashy ankles. Heart cracked open like a window in spring.

And for once, she didn't feel behind. She didn't feel late to the journey.

She felt *present.*

Like maybe she hadn't missed her purpose at all; she just hadn't looked in the right direction.

The next morning, she missed the bus on purpose. The glass on the auto parts store had been fixed. She just sat there, listening to the corner come alive.

A boy trying to flip on a busted skateboard. A man humming while twisting his daughter's hair. The wind making the flags outside the corner store flutter like somebody was clapping for no reason. And that's when it hit her: she wasn't lost. She wasn't an onion or a cake, but nonetheless, she was layered.

And maybe her purpose wasn't buried deep inside some expensive book or silent retreat. Maybe it was here, in the hood, at the bus stop, watching people *be.*

Watching herself *be.*

That night she wrote, *"Finding myself didn't require leaving my block. Just leaving behind the idea that I had to become someone else."*

"Maybe purpose ain't somewhere else. Maybe it's right here — and I'm the one who finally showed up."

CHAPTER 6: WHEN YOU DON'T EVEN KNOW YOU'RE LOST

Nobody told her purpose could feel like folding socks. Like it was showing up to the same job, drinking the same coffee, smiling at the same security guard, and wondering if the sky was always this gray.

She thought purpose would sparkle.

She thought it would strut in, demand applause, and flip her life like a renovation show.

But most days? Purpose came in sweatpants.

It was there when she didn't hit snooze. It was in the way she returned her shopping cart. In how she asked folks how they were —and meant it.
It was a rhythm. A practice. A whole lot of repetition with occasional glimpses of glory.

See, nobody puts routine on the vision board.

They show the end game, the TED Talk, the glow-up, the soft life.

But not the Tuesdays when you still feel crusty, the Wednesdays when you doubt everything, or the Thursdays when your only win was not crying during a Zoom call.

She had to learn the hard way. Purpose ain't always pretty. Sometimes it's brushing your teeth when depression says don't. Sometimes it's eating leftovers and being grateful. Sometimes it's showing up to the thing you said you'd do, even when no one claps.

One Monday, she sat at her desk and typed the same sentence five different ways. Her boss never noticed. Her inbox couldn't smother her thoughts. And lunch was a bag of seven bitters and vibes.

She went home feeling invisible.

But as she walked past her neighbor's door, a little girl waved and said, *"You smell like bubblegum."*

She laughed. Didn't even wear perfume that day. Maybe it was the spirit of sweetness hanging on her.

For some reason, that hit deeper than it should've. Because sometimes purpose shows up not to wow you. It shows up to remind you. You're still here. You still matter. You still have a scent of sweetness—even when the world feels stale.

She thought about quitting the journey. Not dramatically. Just slowly. Quietly. Like slipping out the back door of a party where no one noticed you came.

But every time she tried, something whispered, *"Keep going. This is still holy."*

So she leaned into the mundane. Started lighting a candle while washing dishes. Played jazz while cleaning her room. Gave herself gold stars for doing regular things.

Woke up? Made a real breakfast? Texted back even though she didn't feel like talking?

One day, she bought a planner. Not to make plans to take over the world, just to track her daily glimmers. She wrote things like:

Didn't scroll Instagram for 2 hours… Growth!
Spoke kindly to myself in the mirror… Queen behavior.
Didn't compare my life to Skylar's today… Priceless.

The planner became proof that purpose was moving, even when it felt stuck.

And the boredom? It started to feel like peace in disguise. There was a stretch of days where nothing *"happened."*

No epiphanies. No drama. Just vibes.

And in that stretch, she realized she was healing. Because before, silence felt like failure. Now, it felt like rest. Miss Wanda at the bus stop said it best:

"Baby, don't confuse peace with nothingness. Sometimes the blessing is in the boring."

That line stayed in her chest like a song lyric.

She stopped looking for fireworks and started listening for whispers. Like when her favorite song came on shuffle right when she needed it. Or when her grandma's soup tasted like a memory. Or when her laugh surprised her. Loud, joyful, and unfiltered. All of that was purpose.

Not glamorous. Not monetized. But real.

And then came the moment she realized what wasn't purpose:

Performing for love.
Mistaking intimacy for identity.
Confusing being touched with being seen.

She used to think that maybe, just maybe, if she laid down with the right someone, she'd rise up with herself. Like the act could plant something in her, some seed of truth. But she knew it wouldn't be that. It would leave her emptier. Like renting a hotel room inside her own body, only to find the sheets on the other side had already gone cold.

Sex, when it ain't sacred, can make you feel like a background character in your own story.

She remembered lying next to a man who barely remembered her nickname, staring at the ceiling thinking:

"Is this it? Is this all I am?"

That was the turning point. Because the truth is, purpose don't come from being chosen. It don't live in someone else's bedroom. It don't bloom just because someone called you pretty in the dark. Then she started asking herself:

Would I still want this if I knew it wasn't love?
Would I still say yes if I wasn't afraid to say no?

She realized she wasn't searching for a man. She was searching for herself—and for Yahweh. And for too long, she'd looked for her reflection in someone else's eyes. But now?

Now she was holding her own mirror. She saw beauty in her own slow and solitary becoming. She saw worth that didn't come with a text back. She saw the holiness in holding herself through the loneliness.

Purpose didn't ask her to prove herself in someone's bed. It asked her to return to herself.

Fully. Freely. Without shame.

She stopped waiting to be seen and started watching herself. Not to criticize, but to witness. To say, *"You're doing it. You're showing up."*

Purpose didn't knock loudly. It showed up like a whisper in the stretch marks. Like a psalm in the sink water. Like an old song she didn't know she needed. She wrote one last line in her planner:

"I am not a hiding place for someone else's confusion. I am a home for my own becoming."

And in that line, she found a kind of quiet thunder. A power not found in performance, but in presence. Because purpose ain't about who wants you. It's about how deeply you honor yourself.

CHAPTER 7: SOMETIMES PURPOSE LOOK LIKE A MESSY BUN AND AN ATTITUDE

She used to think walking in purpose meant floating—waking up one day glowing, sipping matcha and speaking in affirmations with the patience of a preschool teacher and the poise of Nina Simone.

But lately?

Purpose looked like an oversized hoodie, a messy bun halfway falling, and an attitude just spicy enough to keep folks from trying her spirit before 10 a.m.

It was a survival task. It was *"don't talk to me until I pray"* energy. It was *"I'm here, but I didn't have to be, so let's keep it cute."*

But she was learning that even in the mess, there was maintenance. Upkeep wasn't about impressing anyone; it was about honoring the temple Yahweh gave her.

Brushing her edges, cleaning her space, moisturizing her knees with Alchemist Tinq's whipped body butter—even when no one would see them—was sacred business.

That was holiness in action.

One morning, she caught her reflection in the bus window. Her edges weren't laid. Her bag was mismatched. Her face said, *"Ask me one more dumb question."*

And yet... she looked powerful.

Not because she had it all together, but because she showed up anyway.

See, nobody tells you that purpose sometimes rolls out of bed annoyed. That the girl walking in destiny still gets cramps, still has to pluck chin hairs, and still gets mad when folks eat her lunch at work.

Purpose ain't pristine. Sometimes it's loud. Sometimes it's tired. Sometimes it comes with chipped nail polish and coconut oil stains on your shirt.

She started noticing it in other women too.

The mama dragging her toddler and still managing to look like royalty in Crocs and a bonnet. The girl at the laundromat lip-syncing to Tamela Mann like it was her Tiny Desk concert. The auntie who ran a daycare by day, baked pies by night, and still had time to send out encouraging texts on Sundays.

None of them looked like the Instagram version of *"living in pur-*

pose." But they were it.

Walking, talking, breathing purpose in sweatsuits and slides, smelling like shea butter and resilience.

There was one Tuesday morning in particular. She was running late. Hair tied up with a sock. Phone at 3%. And as she walked out the door, her neighbor's child pointed at her and said, *"You look like a superhero!"*

She blinked.

This?

This walking contradiction of dry lips and unpaid bills—while pulling out chapstick from Alchemist Tinq's like it was armor.

But maybe that's exactly what purpose looked like.

Unfiltered. Unbothered. Undeniably present.

She used to think she had to *"fix herself"* to be worthy of purpose. Now she knew better.

Purpose didn't wait for perfect skin. It showed up in stretch marks, chipped nails, and voices that crack when they pray too hard. Purpose looked like sweat. Like sass. Like a stare that says, *"Stop lying to yourself, sis."*

But she also knew: upkeep was part of holiness too.

That wiping down the bathroom mirror, trimming her nails, lighting a candle just to say *"I matter today"*—that was sacred maintenance. Her outer world deserved the same care her inner healing got. Keeping it together wasn't vanity. It was reverence.

She began keeping a *"baddie blessings"* list. Things that weren't traditional wins but felt like sacred self-care:

Didn't explain myself today.
Wore the outfit I liked, not what made others comfortable.
Said no with my chest.

And right next to it, she wrote scripture and sass side by side:

"I am fearfully and wonderfully made." – Psalm 139:14
"And highly unlikely to deal with your nonsense today." – Me

She realized that sometimes, purpose is just holding on to your peace with missing nails and a dollar store wig cap.

Sometimes it's correcting folks who say your name wrong. Sometimes it's not answering that text. Sometimes it's eating your fries in silence while someone tries to trauma-dump during your lunch break.

And yeah, sometimes she had an attitude. But that attitude wasn't bitterness. It was boundaries. It was dignity. It was divine protection wrapped in side-eye.

She didn't have to smile to be holy. Didn't have to be soft-spoken to be sacred. Didn't have to look like she had it all together to actually be on the right path.

She was made in the image of Elohim—with hips, wits, opinions, and the ability to pivot mid-sentence if somebody tried her.

And every time she did the work on herself, for herself, she knew she wasn't just walking in purpose. She was "*living*" it.

Even when her bun was lopsided. Even when she forgot her earrings. Even when she had to pray three times not to cuss somebody out.

Because even on the rough days, she still chose to show up with care.

And that—more than anything else—was holy.

CHAPTER 8: I THOUGHT MY PURPOSE WAS TO BE A BAD EXAMPLE

There was a time when she thought her only role in life was to serve as a cautionary tale. Like she was here to make the wrong turns, so others wouldn't have to.

She'd mess up out loud, and folks would point and whisper like she was the end of a *"Don't do this"* PSA. Her report cards, her relationships, her random meltdowns in Target parking lots—where someone once told her to go to Walmart if she wanted to act like that—all got filed under:

"Exhibit A: What Not To Be."

She wore shame like perfume, over-applied, but expected. Smiled through it. Even made jokes about it. Because if she laughed first, nobody else could use her story to bruise her spirit.

It started young.

Teachers said she was *"distracted."* Family called her *"unique."* Neighbors said, *"That one's gonna be trouble."*

And so, trouble she became. Not because it fit her, but because no one ever offered her a better script.

She learned to dance in dysfunction like it was a talent show. Got good at rebound relationships and rebound plans. Made chaos look like confidence. Even labeled herself the black sheep, like it was a flex.

"Y'all don't gotta worry about me, I'm the one who messes up for the whole family."

It was a mask. Heavy, cracked, but familiar.

Then came her niece. Just seven years old. Tugged on her hoodie one day and said, *"Auntie, I wanna be like you when I grow up."*

That sentence hit like a drum in a silent room.

She froze. She thought to herself, *"What exactly was I modeling?"*

She wanted to say, *"Baby, aim higher. I'm still tryna untangle my own mess."*

But her niece wasn't asking about perfection.

She said, *"You always say what you mean. And you're funny. And you make the best noodles."*

Simple. Pure. Unfiltered admiration.

That night she had wept. Real tears. The kind that don't need music or candles, just you, your floor, and your truth. Because maybe she *had* been a mess. But maybe that wasn't the whole story.

She started revisiting her so-called *"failures."* Not to relive the pain, but to look for purpose in the wreckage.

That relationship that wrecked her? Taught her what love isn't. The job she lost because she snapped back one too many times? Showed her she wasn't made to be silenced, but she needed to be better. The years she spent trying to blend in? Proved Yahweh didn't design her for dilution.

She started piecing together a new picture.

Not a highlight reel. Not a sob story. A mosaic.

Because here's the thing: *a broken mirror still reflects.*

She started speaking differently.

When her younger cousin vented about messing up, she didn't say, *"Girl, why'd you do that?"* She said, *"I've been there. Let's clean it up together."*

When someone tried to label her again, she said, *"I'm not a mistake, I'm a remix."*

Whole new version. Still bumpin'. Still blessed. And slowly, she stopped apologizing for her path. Stopped shrinking her testimony. Stopped turning her redemption into a punchline.

She wasn't a *"bad example."*

She was a lived example. Proof that Elohim uses all things, even the raggedy chapters, to build legacy.

She got bold. Not loud-bold. Aligned-bold.

Started walking into rooms like her story was a scroll. Didn't edit out the embarrassing parts. Didn't flinch when someone brought up her past. Just nodded and said, *"Yeah, I remember that version of me. She taught me everything."*

She even started mentoring folks who used to side-eye her. Not on purpose, it just happened. People felt safe around her messiness. Safe to cry. Safe to question. Safe to not have it together.

She became someone people called when they wanted real answers, not Pinterest quotes. Because she *got it.*

She knew what it meant to be in the dark and not know which way was up. She knew the shame of relapse. The ache of forgiving yourself at 2 a.m. And still, showing up while in turmoil.

Purpose didn't skip over her. It just waited.
Waited for her to stop disqualifying herself.
Waited for her to look in the mirror and say, *"Even this version of me is worthy."*

Waited for her to stop auditioning for acceptance.

And when she finally stood still, when she unclenched her spirit and listened, she heard it: a soft, steady voice saying, *"You are mine. I can use all of you."*

Now, when someone calls her *"the one who used to be wild,"* she laughs. *"Still a little wild, baby girl—but now it's tempered."*

CHAPTER 9: WHITE GIRL PROBLEMS? NAH, IT'S EVERYONE

I used to think only white girls got to find themselves.

That finding your *"truth"* was a privilege—one that came with therapy co-pays, Himalayan salt lamps, and enough savings to fall apart and still pay rent.

I thought purpose was oat-milk exclusive—reserved for women who could afford to fall apart beautifully.

Skylar could cry in Whole Foods and call it a spiritual awakening. Madison could break up with her man and book a healing retreat in Sedona.

Meanwhile, I was rationing ramen and telling myself it wasn't hunger—it was intermittent fasting.

I thought finding purpose was a luxury—that people like me didn't get to go on sabbaticals. They took naps. They cried in public bathrooms. They faked peace at family reunions.

But then something wild happened.

I started meeting people like me—people who looked like me, moved like me, and prayed in their grandma's voice— who were walking in purpose too.

Not the curated kind. The gritty kind. Like:

There was Mr. Nettles, who ran a restaurant and prayed over pickles. A teenager who rapped poetry on the train platform between shifts. A mama who made joy out of Kool-Aid packets and gospel music on repeat.

Purpose wasn't out of reach. It was out loud.

It was everywhere once I actually started paying attention. Then it hit me: *purpose ain't about aesthetic. It's about assignment.*
You don't need yoga pants and a reusable water bottle. You need ears to hear when the Ruach HaKodesh whispers—and the guts to move when Yahweh says, *"Go."*

It's not a white girl problem. It's a human problem.

And the real tragedy is that so many folks like me didn't even know they had permission to ask the question. They were taught to survive, not search. To endure, not expand. To give, not grow.

But growth is holy. And searching is sacred.

I realized I wasn't crazy for craving more. I wasn't spoiled for asking, *"Why am I here?"*

That question was my birthright.

I remembered what someone once told me:

"Your ancestors didn't survive so you could spend your life only being tired."

So I stopped apologizing.
Stopped thinking my curiosity made me selfish.
Stopped thinking my dreams had to look like someone else's highlight reel.

Because my purpose wasn't rented. It was rooted.

I started claiming it out loud.

"I'm here for more."
"I'm not just clocking in and clocking out—I'm clocked into destiny."
"My melanin is not a mistake. My mission is not optional. My mess is not disqualifying."

I realized *"white"* girls didn't own purpose. Maybe they just had the better marketing. And honestly? That's fine. Because purpose doesn't require a brand. It requires obedience.

Now, when Skylar and I are sipping matcha and talking about inner peace, I don't roll my eyes at her.

I nod.

Because *"yeah, 'I AM TELLING YOU', peace is beautiful."*

And so is shouting scriptures in a headscarf.
So is catching the Spirit while frying chicken.
So is rocking thrift-store shoes and still walking like you're on holy ground.

It's everyone. It's the boy in detention who writes poems in the margins. It's the elder who remembers the old songs and sings them into the soil. It's the girl with tattoos, tears, and a testimony. It's the uncle who fixes bikes for free because it's how he meditates.

It's **YOU**. It's always been **YOU**.

I used to think my purpose was to be a bad example. Now I knows my purpose is to be an example.

Of what grace looks like in gold hoops.
Of what healing looks like in a hoodie.
Of what Yahweh's favor looks like when it's not filtered.

I walk different now. Not because my life got easy, but because it got clearer. The ache in my chest wasn't shame—it was the echo of heaven calling my name. That I didn't miss the boat—I am on time.

Sailing. Anchored. Divine.

Skylar looked at me and said, *"Girl, you different now."*
I smiled and said, *"I'm not different. I'm delivered."*

My name RAJ.

So yeah… White girl problems? Nah, baby. It's everyone.

But don't get it twisted—not every Skylar has the potential to float through life, and not every Raj grew up less fortunate.

But everyone have a **PURPOSE.**
YOU just have to find **YOURS.**

THE LABEL

People love to label pain.

If it cries with mascara running, it's "white girl problems."

If it cries behind closed doors, it's "man up."

If it cries in church, it's "pray harder."

If it cries in silence, it's "attention-seeking."

We categorize struggle the way we categorize playlists.

By genre. By aesthetic. By stereotype.

But pain doesn't check race before it enters a body.

Confusion doesn't verify your background before it wrecks your sense of self.

And purpose — real purpose — doesn't discriminate.

This story isn't about white girls.

It isn't about Black girls.

It isn't about men.

It isn't about women.

It's about the lie we all believe

www.ingramcontent.com/pod-product-compliance
Lightning Source LLC
Chambersburg PA
CBHW030814090426
42737CB00010B/1274